# THE
# NO-SUGAR
# COOKBOOK

ADDIE GONSHOROWSKI

Cover and Illustrations by Robin Denmark Koontz

No Sugar — No Honey
No Fructose — No Saccharin

## AD-DEE PUBLISHERS, INC.

# ACKNOWLEDGEMENT

I DEDICATE THIS BOOK TO
MY GRANDCHILDREN
TIM • SUSAN • GARY


WITH SPECIAL THANKS
to my husband and children
for their encouragement

PUBLISHED BY:   AD-DEE PUBLISHERS, INC.,
P.O. BOX 5426-SL83
EUGENE, OREGON 97405

ISBN: 0-9600982-7

# CONTENTS

BARS .................................................... 43
BREADS .................................................. 7
BUTTERS & SPREADS ............................ 52
CAKES .................................................. 21
COOKIES ............................................... 34
CONFECTIONS ...................................... 45
DESSERTS ............................................. 56
FILLINGS ............................................... 19
FROSTINGS ........................................... 33
FROZEN DESSERTS ............................... 64
GELATINS ............................................. 58
ICE CREAM ........................................... 60
JAMS & JELLIES ................................... 50
MILKSHAKE .......................................... 63
MUFFINS ............................................... 7
PIES & CRUSTS .................................73 - 87
POPSICLE .............................................. 63
PUDDINGS ............................................ 67
SALADS ................................................ 93
SALAD DRESSINGS ...........................93 - 96
SAUCES ................................................ 90
SYRUPS ................................................ 92
TEA BREADS ......................................... 9
TOPPINGS ........................................70 - 86
YEAST BREADS ..................................... 17

TO ORDER ADDITIONAL COPIES, SEE PAGE 100

DISTRIBUTORS • BOOKSTORES • FUNDRAISERS
Write for additional discounts to:

AD-DEE PUBLISHERS, INC.
2736 Lincoln Street
Post Office Box 5426-SL83
Eugene, Oregon 97405

# INTRODUCTION

Recipes in this book are intended to help add variety to the diet without use of sugar, honey, fructose or saccharin.

Each person has different desires and tastes concerning how sweet desserts should be.

Allow yourself time to adjust to foods that are not as sweet, as it may take several weeks to become accustomed to less sweet foods.

Once a person adjusts to less sweet foods, they generally prefer them over the sugar loaded desserts.

I suggest you try several different desserts before deciding. Also, allow time to become adjusted to this type of less sweet dessert.

Very few cookbooks have been published without the use of sugar, honey, fructose or saccharin. Therefore, I am pleased to be able to offer this book and hope you will enjoy all the recipes in it.

— ADDIE GONSHOROWSKI

# NOTICE

The recipes in this book have no added sugar, honey, fructose or saccharin type sweeteners.

All recipes with sweeteners were tested with "EQUAL® brand low-calorie sweetener".

The recipes have been newly created and should be allowable in most sugar restricted diets . . .

Each individual should follow their own diet and if in doubt discuss the use of any recipes with their DIET COUNSELOR.

Avoid any recipes that contain ingredients not allowed in the diet unless substitutions can be made to meet the allowances.

Approximate exchanges are given as a general guide for those persons that follow the exchange system in their diet.

AUTHOR/PUBLISHER assumes NO LIABILITY for an individual's diet allowances. No liability will be assumed for any exchanges that are not correct or exact OR for any ingredients that may not be acceptable in any person or persons diet.

SATISFACTION GUARANTEED in the amount of purchase price of this book only.

NO LIABILITIES OF ANY KIND WILL BE ASSUMED BY EITHER AUTHOR or PUBLISHER.

# GENERAL INFORMATION

## HOW TO WARM FOODS

OVEN METHOD

Wrap food in aluminum foil and place in hot oven for few minutes or until nicely warmed.

MICROWAVE

Place food on plate and cover lightly with paper towel. Warm on high 10 to 15 seconds for 1 or 2 servings. Adjust time to number of servings and if food is frozen it may take few seconds longer. DO NOT WRAP & do not leave in more than few seconds as too long will destroy sweetening.

## KEEP FOODS
## REFRIGERATED OR FROZEN

Foods made without sugar must be kept refrigerated or frozen. Follow instructions on recipe.

WHOLE WHEAT FLOUR may be substituted in part in some of the recipes that use all-purpose flour.

Use 1 tblsp per cup less of whole wheat flour and do not substitute more than 1/2 of the flour. Do not expect the same results, as texture and flavor will not be as good.

## NON-SACCHARIN
## EQUAL® BRAND SWEETENER

| | |
|---|---|
| 1 pkt = 2 tsp sugar | 4½ pkts = 3 tbsp sugar |
| 1½ pkts = 1 tbsp sugar | 6 pkts = ¼ cup sugar |
| 3 pkts = 2 tbsp sugar | 8 pkts = $1/3$ cup sugar |

# BREADS

# & MUFFINS

# APPLE SPICE BREAD

¾ cup raisins
½ cup water
¼ cup butter
¼ cup dry milk powder
2 medium eggs, slightly beaten
½ cup apple juice
5 tblsp raisin liquid (from cooking raisins)
2 cups flour
2 tsp baking powder
½ tsp soda
½ tsp salt
1 tsp cinnamon
¼ tsp nutmeg
$1/8$ tsp cloves
¼ cup nuts, chopped fine
¾ cup apple, peeled & chopped fine

IN SAUCEPAN: Combine raisins and water and simmer about 5 minutes. Drain into cup and set aside.

CREAM butter and dry milk; ADD eggs, juice, raisin liquid and beat well.

MIX TOGETHER dry ingredients and beat into butter mixture.

MIX IN raisins and apples.

POUR into 2 small greased loaf pans and let set 20 minutes.

BAKE 350 degrees 25 to 35 minutes or until toothpick comes out clean and bread is light brown. SET on rack. MAKES 24 slices.

SERVE warmed slices with Applebutter (see index).

APPROXIMATE EXCHANGE: 1 Slice = 1/2 Bread — 1/3 Fruit — 3/4 Fat

# BLUEBERRY BREAD

¼ cup butter
2 medium eggs
¾ cup orange juice
2½ tblsp water
2 cups flour
2 tsp baking powder
½ tsp soda
½ tsp salt
2½ tsp cinnamon
¼ tsp allspice
1 tsp grated orange rind
¼ cup nuts, chopped fine
1 cup Blueberries

BEAT butter, eggs, juice & water until well blended.

MIX together flour, baking powder, soda, salt, cinnamon, allspice, orange rind & nuts.

BEAT into creamed mixture. FOLD in blueberries.

POUR into 2 small greased loaf pans and let set 20 minutes.

BAKE 350 degrees 40 to 45 minutes or to done.

COOL or rack. SERVE warm slices with Orange spread (see index)

MAKES 24 slices.

STORE in freezer.

APPROXIMATE EXCHANGE: 1 Slice = 1/2 Bread — Trace Fruit — 2/3 Fat

NOTE If using frozen berries, FOLD in while frozen to prevent coloring of batter.

# ORANGE DATE BREAD

¼ cup butter
2 medium eggs, beaten
¾ cup Orange juice
3 tblsp water
2 cups sifted flour
2 tsp baking powder
½ tsp soda
½ tsp salt
1 tsp cinnamon
¼ cup nuts, chopped fine
20 dates, cut up very fine

CREAM butter, Add eggs, juice and water.

MIX flour, baking powder, soda, salt, and cinnamon and add to butter mixture beating thoroughly.

ADD nuts, and dates and mix well.

POUR into 2 small greased loaf pans and let set for 20 minutes before baking.

BAKE 350 degrees for 30 to 40 minutes or until tooth pick comes out clean and bread is lightly browned.

COOL or racks. Warm slices before serving.

STORE in freezer.

MAKES 24 slices.

APPROXIMATE EXCHANGE: 1 Slice = 1/2 Bread — 1/2 Fruit — 2/3 Fat

# PINEAPPLE DATE BREAD

¼ cup butter
2 medium eggs
1 cup Less 1 tblsp pineapple juice, unsweetened
2 cups all-purpose flour
½ cup unprocessed bran (optional)
2 tsp baking powder
½ tsp soda
½ tsp salt
1½ tsp cinnamon
¼ cup nuts, chopped fine
¾ cup crushed unsweetened pineapple (drained very well)
20 dates, chopped fine

CREAM butter, ADD eggs & juice and beat.

COMBINE flour, bran, baking powder, soda, salt, cinnamon & nuts.

BEAT into butter mixture and add pineapple and dates. MIX well.

POUR into greased medium size loaf pan and let set 20 minutes.

BAKE 350 degrees 30 to 40 minutes or until toothpick comes out clean and bread is light brown.

COOL on rack and turn out of pans.

WARM slices before serving.

STORE in freezer.

MAKES 24 slices.

APPROXIMATE EXCHANGE: 1 Slice = 1/2 Bread — 1/2 Fruit — 2/3 Fat

# PRUNE BREAD

½ cup prunes
1 cup water
¼ cup butter
¼ cup dry milk powder
2 medium eggs
¾ cup cool prune juice (from cooking prunes)
2 cups all-purpose flour
2 tsp baking powder
½ tsp soda
½ tsp salt
2 tsp cinnamon
¼ tsp cloves
¼ cup nuts, chopped fine

COOK prunes in water 5 minutes; Drain into measuring cup and save 3/4 cup. CHOP prunes.

CREAM butter & milk powder; ADD eggs, prune juice and prunes. Beat to blend.

COMBINE dry ingredients and nuts and beat into creamed mixture

POUR into 2 greased small loaf pans and let set 20 minutes.

BAKE 350 degrees about 30 to 35 minutes to light brown and tested done with toothpick.

SET on rack.

SERVE warm slices with prune butter (see index).

STORE in freezer.

MAKES 24 slices.

APPROXIMATE EXCHANGE: 1 Slice = 1/2 Bread — 1/3 Fruit — 2/3 Fat

# RAISIN BREAD

1 1/3 cup flour, sifted
2¼ tsp baking powder
½ tsp salt
1 tsp cinnamon
¼ tsp cloves
¼ tsp nutmeg
¼ cup chopped nuts
1 cup raisins, chopped
1 medium egg, beaten
½ cup milk
2 tblsp melted shortening

MIX flour, baking powder, salt, cinnamon, cloves, nutmeg and nuts.

STIR in raisins.

COMBINE egg, milk, shortening and add to dry mixture just to moist.

BAKE in greased 4" x 7" pan 350 degree oven about 45 to 55 minutes or to done.

SET on rack and turn out in 10 minutes.

SERVE slightly warm slices.

MAKES 10 slices.

APPROXIMATE EXCHANGE: 1 Slice = 1 Bread — 3/4 Fruit — 1 Fat

# APPLE MUFFINS

½ cup + 1 tblsp all-purpose flour
¾ cup whole wheat flour
2¼ tsp baking powder
¼ tsp salt
1 tsp cinnamon
½ tsp cloves
1 small apple
1 medium egg
½ cup skim milk
¼ cup salad oil
½ tsp vanilla
½ cup dates, chopped fine
¼ cup nuts, chopped fine


MIX flours, baking powder, salt, cinnamon, and cloves.

PEEL & grate apple and add to flour mixture.

BEAT together egg, milk, oil and vanilla and add to dry mixture to just moisten.

ADD dates and nuts.

BAKE in 8 greased muffin cups 400 degrees about 18 to 20 minutes or to done.

SERVE warm with Applebutter (see index).

APPROXIMATE EXCHANGE: 1 Muffin = 1 Bread — 1 Fruit — 2 Fat

# CORN FLAKE SPICE MUFFINS

2 cups flour
3 tsp baking powder
½ tsp salt
2 tsp cinnamon
½ cup dry milk

2 medium eggs, beaten
⅔ cup skim milk
¼ cup cooking oil
1 cup corn flakes, no sugar added
1 cup raisins, chop fine

MIX flour, baking powder, salt, cinnamon & dry milk.

COMBINE eggs, skim milk & oil & add to dry ingredients . . . stir just to moisten . . . FOLD in corn flakes and raisins.

BAKE in 12 paper lined muffin cups 400 degrees 15 minutes or until done. SERVE WARM.

APPROXIMATE EXCHANGE: 1 Muffin = 1¹/₅ Bread — 1/6 Meat — 2/3 Fruit — 1 Fat

# BLUEBERRY ORANGE MUFFINS

1½ cup whole wheat flour
½ tsp salt
3 tsp baking powder
½ tsp cinnamon
¼ tsp allspice
¼ tsp nutmeg
2 medium eggs, beaten

¼ cup oil
¾ cup unsweet orange juice
1 tsp grated orange rind
¼ cup nuts
1 cup blueberries

MIX dry ingredients. COMBINE eggs, oil, juice & rind and add to dry ingredients until almost moist. FOLD in blueberries & nuts

BAKE in 18 well greased muffin tins 400 degrees 20 to 25 minutes to done.

APPROXIMATE EXCHANGE: 1 Muffin = 1/2 Bread — 1/5 Fruit — 1 Fat

# BASIC BREAD DOUGH

2 cups skim milk
¼ cup raisins
2 tsp salt
½ cup shortening
2 pkg active dry yeast
¼ cup lukewarm water
6 cups flour
4 egg yolks

2 DAYS BEFORE BAKING: MIX raisins and milk and let set in refrigerator.

ON MORNING OF BAKING:

DRAIN milk into saucepan (discard raisins).

SCALD milk and add salt and shortening. Let cool to warm.

IN SEPARATE BOWL: Soften yeast in water.

IN LARGE MIXING BOWL:

BEAT into milk mixture 1 cup flour and the yolks. ADD yeast and beat in; Then add about 3 to 4 cups more flour with beater.

WHEN beater can not handle dough work in the rest of flour with large spoon or hand slowly until dough is no longer sticky.

COVER BOWL with a towel and let rise in warm place about 85 to 90 degrees to double.

USE THIS DOUGH for making cinnamon rolls, clover-leaf rolls, filled jam rolls, etc.

HINT: The electric oven is a perfect place to let bread rise . . . TURN oven on for few seconds . . . THEN shut off and place bowl with dough on rack . . . Be sure oven does not get over 90 degrees.

# CINNAMON ROLLS

1 Recipe basic bread dough (see index)
3 tblsp butter
cinnamon
1 cup raisins, chopped fine

AFTER bread dough has risen; Punch down and place on lightly floured board.

ROLL to ¼'' thick in rectangle.

SPREAD dough with butter and sprinkle with cinnamon, then raisins; Press raisins in dough lightly.

ROLL up like a jelly roll and seal edges.

WITH sharp knife or with a thread cut into 36 rolls. PLACE in greased pans. Leave space for raising & brush with melted butter between rolls lightly to prevent sticking together.

PLACE in warm place about 85 degrees and let rise to double.

BAKE 350 degrees about 20 minutes. REMOVE & brush tops with milk. REMOVE FROM PANS & let cool on rack.

APPROXIMATE EXCHANGE: 1 Roll = 1 Bread — 1/5 Fruit — 1/3 Fat

# DATE NUT ROLLS

1 cup pitted chopped dates
¾ cup water
1 tsp lemon juice
1 tsp cinnamon
¼ cup nuts, chopped fine

COOK dates, water & juice to soft; BLEND to smooth. ADD cinnamon & nuts.

FOLLOW instructions above for rolling dough & spread date filling on dough. PROCEED with raising & baking instructions as above.

# FILLED ROLLS

1 recipe basic bread dough (see index)

AFTER bread has risen; Punch down and roll out to about 1/2''
thick. Cut with donut cutter and stretch to oblong so that centers
just touch. PLACE on greased cookie sheets and let rise to double
in warm place 85 to 90 degrees.

BAKE 350 degrees about 15 minutes or to light brown . . RE-
MOVE from oven and brush lightly with melted butter . . . FILL
centers.

# PRUNE FILLING

1 cup pitted prunes, cooked and drained
½ tsp cinnamon
½ tsp grated lemon rind
Non-Saccharin sweetener to = ¼ cup sugar

MASH prunes and add rest of ingredients.

APPROXIMATE EXCHANGE: 1 tblsp = 2/3 Fruit

# APPLE FILLING

1 cup peeled sliced thick apples
¼ tsp cinnamon
½ tsp lemon juice
Non-Saccharin sweetener to taste

COOK apples and drain well. MASH and simmer to thicken.

SET off heat 20 minutes and add rest of ingredients.

APPROXIMATE EXCHANGE: 1 tblsp = 3/4 Fruit

# WHOLE WHEAT ROLLS

3½ cup whole wheat flour
2 pkg active dry yeast
1 cup raisin water (see index)
⅓ cup dry milk powder
1 cup 2% milk
3 tsp salt
3 tblsp shortening
2 medium eggs, beat slightly
3 - 3½ cups all-purpose flour

MIX together whole wheat flour and yeast.

IN SAUCEPAN combine raisin water, milk powder, 2% milk, salt and shortening and heat to melt shortening stirring constantly. COOL to lukewarm.

ADD to whole wheat flour & yeast mixture; ADD eggs and beat at low speed with electric mixer for 1/2 minute; SET mixer to high and beat 3 minutes.

BY HAND stir in enough all-purpose flour to make a stiff dough.

TURN out on floured board and knead until smooth and not sticky about 10 minutes.

PLACE in greased bowl turning once and cover with cloth; PLACE in warm place 85 to 90 degrees and let rise to double. PUNCH DOWN and let set 10 minutes.

SHAPE into 24 rolls and place on greased sheets; COVER and place in warm place to rise.

BAKE 400 degree oven 15 to 20 minutes.

BEST served warm.

APPROXIMATE EXCHANGE: 1 Roll = 1 Bread

# CAKES

# APPLESAUCE CAKE

½ cup butter
2 medium eggs, slightly beaten
1 tsp vanilla
1½ cup thick applesauce, unsweetened
2 cups flour
2 tsp baking powder
½ tsp soda
¼ tsp nutmeg
¼ tsp cloves
1 tsp cinnamon
1 cup dates, chopped fine
¼ cup nuts, chopped fine

CREAM butter; ADD eggs, vanilla, applesauce and beat well.

MIX flour, baking powder, soda, nutmeg, cloves & cinnamon.

ADD to creamed mixture and beat well.

ADD dates and nuts.

BAKE in 2 small greased loaf pans 375 degrees 35 to 45 minutes or until toothpick inserted in center comes out clean and cake is nicely browned.

SET on rack 15 minutes and turn out to cool.

SERVE slices warm with Applebutter (see index).

STORE in freezer.

MAKES 24 slices.

APPROXIMATE EXCHANGE: 1 Slice = 1/2 Bread — 3/4 Fruit — 1$^1/_5$ Fat

# BANANA CAKE

1 cup raisins
½ cup water
½ cup butter
¼ cup dry milk powder
3 small bananas, well ripened and mashed
¼ cup raisin liquid (from cooking raisins)
1 tsp vanilla
2 cups all-purpose flour
2 tsp baking powder
1 tsp soda
2 tsp cinnamon
¼ tsp allspice
¼ tsp cloves
1 tsp salt
2 medium eggs, beat lightly
¼ cup nuts, chopped very fine

COOK raisins in water. COOL & drain, save liquid.

CREAM butter and dry milk powder; ADD bananas, raisin liquid & vanilla. BEAT well.

COMBINE dry ingredients and add to butter mixture and beat 3 minutes.

ADD eggs and beat 2 minutes. ADD raisins & nuts.

BAKE in greased 9" x 10" cake pan or 2 small loaf pans 350 degrees about 30 to 40 minutes or to lightly brown and tested done.

SERVE lightly warm with date spread (see index).

STORE IN FREEZER.

MAKES 32 pieces.

APPROXIMATE EXCHANGE: 1 Piece = 1/2 Bread — 1/2 Fruit — 3/4 Fat

# CHERRY CAKE

¼ cup butter
½ cup dry milk powder
1 medium egg, slightly beaten
½ cup cold water
¼ cup skim milk
½ tsp cherry extract
¼ tsp red food coloring
1 cup all-purpose flour
1 tsp cinnamon
2 tsp baking powder
½ tsp salt
$^1/_3$ cup nuts, chopped fine
½ cup canned, unsweet cherries, drained well

CREAM butter & dry milk powder. ADD egg, water, milk, extract and coloring and beat well.

COMBINE dry ingredients and add to creamed mixture and beat to combine well. ADD cherries.

POUR into greased 8" square cake pan and bake 325 degrees about 25 to 30 minutes or to done.

PLACE on rack & proceed with following.

TOPPING
Prepare "Cherry topping" (see index) using 1½ tsp cornstarch.

SPLIT servings of warm cake into dessert dishes and layer with topping.

TOP with whip topping or Ice cream.

APPROXIMATE EXCHANGE: CAKE ONLY 1/16 = 1/2 Bread — 1 Fat

# CHOCOLATE COCONUT CAKE

⅓ cup butter
1 medium egg
½ cup skim milk
¾ tsp vanilla
½ tsp almond extract
2 tsp chocolate extract
1⅓ cup flour
1 tblsp cocoa
2 tsp baking powder
½ tsp soda
2 tblsp nuts, chopped
½ cup moist coconut (see index)

BEAT butter & egg. MIX together milk and flavorings . . . MIX together flour, cocoa, baking powder and soda.

ADD milk & flour mixture to butter mixture alternately beating after each addition.

BEAT 2 minutes on low speed. (Mixture will be thick)

ADD coconut and nuts.

BAKE in 8" square greased cake pan 350 degrees about 25 to 30 minutes or until toothpick inserted in center comes out clean.

BEST served slightly warmed with Cream Cheese chocolate frosting (see index).

MAKES 16 pieces.

APPROXIMATE EXCHANGE: 1 Piece = 2/3 Bread — 1⅓ Fat Plus Frosting

# MAPLE CAKE

1/3 cup dry milk powder
½ cup margarine, melted
1 cup ground raisins
2 medium eggs, slightly beaten
1 tsp maple extract
2 cups flour
1 tsp soda
1 tsp cinnamon
½ tsp nutmeg
¼ tsp cloves
1 cup hot applesauce
¼ cup nuts, chopped fine

CREAM milk powder & margarine.

ADD raisins, eggs and extract. BEAT well.

COMBINE flour, soda, cinnamon, nutmeg and cloves.

ALTERNATELY beat in flour mixture and applesauce into creamed mixture.

ADD nuts.

POUR into greased & floured 8" x 12" cake pan.

BAKE 350 degrees 25 to 35 minutes or until toothpick inserted in
center comes out clean and cake is nicely browned.

REMOVE from oven and place on rack.

SERVE warm pieces with Ice cream or whip topping.

MAKES 24 servings.

APPROXIMATE EXCHANGE: 1 Serving = 1/2 Bread — 1/2
Fruit — 1 Fat

# ORANGE RAISIN CAKE

½ cup skim dry milk powder
¼ cup butter
1 medium egg, beaten
¾ cup orange juice
1 cup flour
1 tsp cinnamon
2 tsp baking powder
½ tsp salt
½ cup raisins, chopped fine
2 tsp grated orange rind
1/3 cup nuts, chopped fine

CREAM milk powder with butter. ADD egg and juice and beat well.

MIX flour, cinnamon, baking powder & salt. ADD raisins & rind and mix well.

STIR dry ingredients into creamed mixture stirring well. STIR in nuts.

POUR into greased loaf pan and bake 325 degrees about 45 minutes or to done.

COOL on rack and remove from pan.

PREPARE TOPPING: MIX 3/4 cup orange juice & 1/4 tsp rum flavoring and heat about 5 minutes.

COOL and add Non-Saccharin sweetener to = 4 tsp sugar.

POKE holes in cake about 1" apart and dribble juice mixture over cake until it is absorbed.

PLACE in refrigerator overnight . . . Warm slightly and serve with whip topping or ice cream.

APPROXIMATE EXCHANGE: 1/12 Cake = 1/2 Bread —1/2 Fruit — 1⅓ Fat

# ORANGE GELATIN CAKE

½ cup skim dry milk powder
¼ cup butter
1 medium egg, beaten
¾ cup orange juice
1 cup flour

1 tsp cinnamon
2 tsp baking powder
½ tsp salt
½ cup raisins, chopped fine
2 tsp grated orange rind
$1/3$ cup nuts, chopped fine

CREAM milk powder & butter. ADD egg and juice and beat well.

MIX flour, cinnamon, baking powder & salt. ADD raisins & rind and mix well. STIR into creamed mixture and add nuts stirring well.

POUR into greased 8" square cake pan and bake 325 degrees 25 to 35 minutes or to done. COOL on rack & poke holes in cake about 1 inch apart.

# ORANGE GELATIN

2½ tsp unflavored gelatin
2 tsp lemon juice
1¼ cup orange juice
Non-Saccharin sweetener to = ¼ cup sugar

IN SAUCEPAN sprinkle gelatin over 1/4 cup juice & let set 10 minutes . . . HEAT to dissolve.

ADD lemon juice and 1 cup orange juice.

ADD sweetener and stir. CHILL to just syrupy.

DRIZZLE over cake slowly to allow absorbing (any gelatin left may be chilled & served).

APPROXIMATE EXCHANGE: 1/12 of Cake = 3/4 Bread — 2/3 Fruit — 1½ Fat

# PINEAPPLE JUICE CAKE

½ cup skim dry milk powder
¼ cup butter
1 medium egg, beaten
¾ cup pineapple juice
½ tsp pineapple flavoring
1 cup flour
2 tsp cinnamon
2 tsp baking powder
½ tsp salt
½ cup chopped dates
$1/3$ cup chopped nuts

CREAM milk powder & butter . . . ADD egg, juice & flavoring.

COMBINE rest of ingredients and stir into creamed mixture.

BAKE in greased loaf pan 325 degrees about 45 minutes or to done.

COOL on rack and remove from pan to serving tray.

TOPPING

MIX 3/4 cup pineapple juice & 1/4 tsp pineapple flavoring and simmer slowly few minutes.

COOL and add Non-Saccharin sweetener to = 5 tsp sugar.

POKE holes in cake about 1" apart and dribble juice over cake until absorbed.

PLACE IN refrigerator and let set to next day . . . Warm slightly and serve with whip topping or ice cream.

APPROXIMATE EXCHANGE: 1/12 Cake = 1/2 Bread − 1 Fruit − $1^{1}/_{3}$ Fat

# PINEAPPLE CAKE

½ cup skim dry milk powder
¼ cup butter
1 medium egg, beaten
½ cup crushed pineapple, drained slightly
½ cup pineapple juice
½ tsp pineapple flavoring
1 cup all-purpose flour
2 tsp cinnamon
2 tsp baking powder
½ tsp salt
½ cup dates, chopped fine
¼ cup nuts, chopped fine

CREAM milk powder & butter. ADD egg, pineapple, juice & flavoring and mix well.

MIX flour, cinnamon, baking powder, salt, dates & nuts.

STIR into creamed mixture and mix well.

BAKE in 8″ square cake pan and bake 325 degrees 25 to 35 minutes or to done. PLACE on rack, and proceed with following:

TOPPING
Prepare "Pineapple topping" (see index)

SPLIT servings of warm cake into dessert dishes and layer with topping; TOP with whip topping or Ice cream.

APPROXIMATE EXCHANGE: 1/16 of Cake = 1/2 Bread — 2/3 Fruit — 1 Fat

VARIATION:

Cake Filling — Follow recipe for cream pie filling (see index) and add crushed drained unsweet pineapple.

# PRUNE CAKE

½ cup nonfat dry milk powder
4 tblsp margarine, softened
1 medium egg, beaten
¾ cup apple juice
1 cup flour, sifted before measuring
1½ tsp baking powder
½ tsp salt
1 tsp cinnamon
12 medium prunes, chopped very fine

CREAM milk powder & margarine; ADD egg & juice.

COMBINE flour, baking powder, salt & cinnamon.

ADD prunes and mix well. STIR dry ingredients into juice mixture & mix well.

BAKE in greased 9 x 5'' loaf pan 325 degrees about 35 to 45 minutes to done.

COOL on rack.

SERVE slightly warm slices with prune frosting below.

APPROXIMATE EXCHANGE: 1/12 of loaf = 1/2 Bread — 3/4 Fruit — Trace Milk — 1 Fat Plus Frosting

# PRUNE FROSTING

BEAT TOGETHER: 6 tblsp cream cheese; 3/4 cup prune butter & Non-Saccharin sweetener to = 2 tblsp sugar. STORE in refrigerator or freezer.

APPROXIMATE EXCHANGE: 1 tblsp = 1/3 Fruit — 1/3 Fat

* * * FOR Prune butter recipe see Index.

# CREAM CHEESE CHOCOLATE FROSTING

½ cup cream cheese, softened
4 tsp milk
Non-Saccharin sweetener to = $^1/_3$ cup sugar
½ tsp salt
2 tsp vanilla
3 tsp chocolate flavoring
¼ cup almonds, sliced

BEAT cheese and milk thoroughly. ADD sweetener, salt, vanilla & chocolate flavor and blend well.

ADD Almonds.

SPREAD on warm cake just before serving.

MAKES 1/2 cup frosting . . . Enough for 8" square cake.

APPROXIMATE EXCHANGE: Complete Recipe = 2/3 Bread — 11$^1/_3$ Fat

# CREAM CHEESE JELLY FROSTING

4 tblsp cream cheese, softened
6 tblsp sugarless jelly or jam of your choice
Non-Saccharin sweetener to your taste

CREAM cheese; ADD jelly and beat to smooth.

ADD sweetener.

STORE in refrigerator & use within 3 days.

# COOKIES

# APPLE DATE DROPS

½ cup dates, cut up
½ cup raisins
1 small apple, chopped
⅓ cup water
⅔ cup apple juice
1 tsp soda
1½ tsp vanilla
½ cup shortening
1 cup flour
1¾ tsp cinnamon
¼ cup nuts, chopped

IN SAUCEPAN: Mix dates, raisins, apple, water, juice, soda & vanilla.

BRING to boil and simmer 3 minutes. COOL.

CREAM shortening and add flour and cinnamon beating to crumbly.

ADD cooked mixture and mix well.

ADD nuts.

CHILL in refrigerator.

DROP on greased teflon cookie sheet.

BAKE 350 degrees on upper middle rack of oven for about 15 to 20 minutes.

LET SET few minutes before removing from pan.

BEST served slightly warmed.

MAKES 30 cookies.

STORE IN FREEZER.

APPROXIMATE EXCHANGE: 1 Cookie = 1/5 Bread — 1/2 Fruit — 1 Fat

# COCONUT MACAROONS

4 egg whites (1/2 cup)
¼ tsp salt
½ tsp vanilla
1 cup moist coconut #2 (see index)
½ cup nuts, chopped fine
½ tsp cinnamon

BEAT whites & salt to very stiff

MIX in vanilla & add coconut, nuts, cinnamon folding in very carefully.

DROP on greased teflon cookie sheets and bake on upper middle rack 325 degrees about 10 minutes or just to light browned.

MAKES 32 cookies.

STORE in refrigerator or freezer.

APPROXIMATE EXCHANGE: 1 Cookie = 1/2 Fat

# APPLESAUCE COOKIES

½ cup cooking oil
1 cup applesauce unsweetened
2 medium eggs, beaten
2 tsp vanilla
1 cup flour
3 tsp cinnamon
½ tsp salt
1 tsp soda
½ tsp nutmeg
¼ tsp cloves
1 cup dry oatmeal
½ cup chopped nuts
1½ cup raisins,
 grind coarsely

BLEND first 4 ingredients . . . MIX and add dry ingredients . . . ADD nuts and raisins.

DROP on greased sheet & bake 375 degrees 10 to 12 minutes . . .

SERVE WARM . . . YIELD 48 cookies

APPROXIMATE EXCHANGE: 1 Cookie = 1/2 Bread — 2/3 Fruit — 1⅓ Fat

# DATE ALMOND COOKIES

½ cup soft butter
6²/₃ tblsp soft cream cheese
1 medium egg
1 cup finely chopped dates
1 tsp almond extract
1¼ cup all-purpose flour
½ tsp salt
½ tsp baking powder
¾ cup quick dry oats


BEAT butter and cream cheese. ADD egg, dates and extract.

SIFT TOGETHER flour, salt, and baking powder.

ADD to butter mixture and beat well. STIR in oats and blend well.

CHILL. Shape into small balls and place on greased cookie sheets and flatten with bottom of glass dipped in flour.

BAKE 375 degrees about 10 to 12 minutes or to lightly brown.

MAKES 42 cookies . . .

STORE IN FREEZER

APPROXIMATE EXCHANGE: 1 Cookie = 1/4 Bread — 1/3 Fruit — 3/4 Fat

# DRIED FRUIT DROPS

½ cup chopped raisins
¼ cup chopped dried apricots
1 cup chopped dates
½ cup chopped nuts
1 cup whole wheat flour
1 tsp cinnamon
1 tsp baking powder
¼ cup cooking oil
3 tsp vanilla
¼ tsp salt
2 medium eggs, slightly beaten

COMBINE fruits . . . Mix flour, cinnamon and baking powder and add to fruit with nuts.

MIX together rest of ingredients and combine both mixtures.

DROP on greased cookie sheet and bake 350 degrees about 8 to 10 minutes (do not allow to overbake).

SERVE slightly warm.

MAKES ABOUT 42 cookies.

APPROXIMATE EXCHANGE: 1 Cookie = 1/6 Bread − 1/2 Fruit − 1/2 Fat

# ORANGE COOKIES

2 cups flour
2 tsp baking powder
½ tsp salt
1½ tsp cinnamon
½ cup unsweetened orange juice
¾ tsp orange flavoring
1 medium egg, slightly beaten
½ cup softened butter
1/3 cups nuts, chopped
¾ cup raisins, chopped


SIFT together flour, baking powder, salt and cinnamon.

MIX together juice, flavoring and egg.

CREAM butter and add flour & liquid alternately.

STIR in nuts and raisins.

DROP on teflon greased cookie sheets and bake 375 degrees on upper middle oven rack for 15 to 20 minutes or to light brown.

SERVE WARM. STORE IN FREEZER. MAKES 30 cookies.

APPROXIMATE EXCHANGE: 1 Cookie = 1/2 Bread — 1/4 Fruit — 1 Fat

# PINEAPPLE COOKIES

2 medium eggs, beaten
²/₃ cup melted margarine, cooled
1 cup skim milk
1 cup crushed, unsweetened pineapple, drained
¹/₃ cup dry milk powder, Non-fat
3 tsp cinnamon
¼ tsp cloves
½ tsp salt
2 tsp baking powder
1½ cups whole wheat flour
1½ cup quick oats
½ cup chopped nuts
½ cup fine chopped dates
1 tsp vanilla


COMBINE eggs, margarine, milk & pineapple.

STIR milk powder, cinnamon, cloves, salt, baking powder, flour & oats together.

ADD dry ingredients to first mixture . . . Add nuts, dates and vanilla.

LET MIXTURE SET ABOUT 15 minutes to set.

Drop on lightly greased cookie sheet and bake 350 degrees 15 to 20 minutes or to done.

SERVE WARM

YIELD: 60 cookies

APPROXIMATE EXCHANGE: 1 Cookie = 1/5 Bread — 1/6 Fruit — 2/3 Fat

41

# TOMATO COOKIES

½ cup margarine,
   melted & cooled
2 medium eggs, beaten
1 can Tomato soup
1½ cups flour
1 tsp baking powder
½ tsp baking soda
2 tsp cinnamon
1 tsp allspice
2 cups quick oats
½ cup chopped nuts
1½ cup raisins

SOAK raisins in Hot water 5 minutes . . . Drain well.

MIX first 3 ingredients . . Stir in dry ingredients, nuts & raisins . . Drop by spoonsful on ungreased cookie sheet . . Dip fork in water & press flat.

Bake 350 degrees about 12 to 15 minutes . . Cool on rack.

Best served warm.

YIELD: 72 cookies.

APPROXIMATE EXCHANGE: 1 Cookie = 1/4 Bread — 1/6 Fruit — 1/2 Fat

# BANANA DATE COOKIES

2 small bananas, mashed
1 cup dates, chopped
$^1/_3$ cup oil
2 cups dry oats
1 tsp cinnamon
¼ tsp cloves
¼ tsp salt
½ cup nuts, chopped
1 tsp vanilla

MIX bananas, dates & oil. ADD oats, spices, salt, nuts & vanilla. MIX LIGHTLY. Let stand for few minutes.

DROP on ungreased cookie sheet. BAKE 350 degrees 20 to 25 minutes or to done.

MAKES 42 cookies.

APPROXIMATE EXCHANGE: 1 Cookie = 1/6 Bread — 1/2 Fruit — 1/2 Fat

# APPLE BARS

1 cup water
1 cup raisins
2 small apples, Peel and chop
¼ cup shortening
2 tsp cinnamon
¼ tsp nutmeg
1 medium egg
1 tsp vanilla
1 cup flour
1 tsp soda
¼ tsp salt
¼ cup nuts

IN SAUCEPAN: Mix water, raisins, apples, shortening, cinnamon & nutmeg.

BRING to boil & simmer 3 minutes. COOL.

IN MIXING BOWL beat egg; ADD vanilla.

COMBINE egg to cooked mixture.

MIX flour, soda, salt & nuts and stir into mixture.

SPREAD in 2 greased 6" x 6" pans.

BAKE 350 degrees about 25 to 30 minutes or until done.

REMOVE from oven and set on rack 10 minutes.

TURN out and cut into 24 bars.

SERVE warm.

STORE IN FREEZER.

APPROXIMATE EXCHANGE: 1 Bar = 1/4 Bread — 1/2 Fruit — 2/3 Fat

# OATMEAL RAISIN BARS

¾ cup margarine, melted
2 medium eggs
2 tsp vanilla
2½ cups uncooked oatmeal
1 cup whole wheat flour
2 tsp baking powder

½ tsp salt
1 tsp cinnamon
¼ tsp allspice
¼ tsp cloves
½ cup nuts, chopped
1 cup raisins, ground coarse

MIX margarine, eggs & vanilla . . . ADD rest of ingredients . . . MIX WELL.

SPREAD on greased cookie sheet 11 x 16″ size.

BAKE 325 degrees 25 to 30 minutes.

CUT into 72 squares . . . SERVE WARM.

APPROXIMATE EXCHANGE: 1 Square = 1/5 Bread — 1/10 Fruit — 2/3 Fat

# MAPLE DATE BARS

2 medium eggs,
  beaten with pinch salt
2 tblsp boiling water
1 cup unbleached flour

1 tsp Maple flavor
2 tsp Baking powder
¼ cup nuts, chop
1 cup dates, chop

Beat eggs & salt to light, Add water & beat.

Sift flour with baking powder & add to mixture.

Add flavoring, nuts & dates.

BAKE in 8″ square greased & floured pan 350 degrees about 15 minutes. Turn out on rack.

CUT into 20 bars. SERVE WARMED.

APPROXIMATE EXCHANGE: 1 Bar = 1/3 Bread — 3/4 Fruit — 1/10 Meat — 1/5 Fat

# CONFECTIONS

# JAMS • JELLIES

# APRICOT DATE BALLS

24 halves dried apricots, cut up
32 dates, chopped
1½ tblsp butter
2½ cups no-sugar corn flakes, crushed
1 tsp cinnamon
¼ cup nuts, chopped fine
Non-Saccharin sweetener to = $^1/_3$ cup sugar

COOK apricots and dates in little water over low heat until tender & water has absorbed.

REMOVE from heat and beat with butter until smooth.

ADD 2 cups corn flake crumbs, cinnamon, nuts, and sweetener and stir well.

ROLL into 24 balls and then roll in rest of crumbs to coat balls.

PLACE on wax paper and chill.

APPROXIMATE EXCHANGE: 1 Ball = 1/6 Bread — 1 Fruit — 1/3 Fat

# COCONUT FRUIT BALLS

½ cup pitted dates
¼ cup raisins
¼ cup pitted prunes (about 6 medium)
2 tblsp nuts, chopped
$^1/_3$ cup moist coconut (see index)

GRIND coarsely the dates, raisins & prunes.

MIX together with nuts and ¼ cup coconut . . .

ROLL into 12 small balls & roll in rest of coconut. CHILL.

APPROXIMATE EXCHANGE: 1 Ball = 1 Fruit — 1/3 Fat

# COCOA FRUIT BALLS

1 tblsp butter
2 tblsp cocoa
1 tblsp water
12 halves dried apricots, chopped very fine
20 dates, chopped very fine
2 tblsp nuts, chopped very fine
8 tblsp moist coconut (see index)
Non-Saccharin sweetener to = 16 tsp sugar

MELT butter and add cocoa and water.

MIX apricots, dates, nuts, and 4 tblsp coconut and the sweetener. ADD butter mixture and stir well.

FORM into 24 balls and roll in rest of coconut.

CHILL and store in refrigerator.

APPROXIMATE EXCHANGE: 1 Ball = 2/3 Fruit — 1/3 Fat

# CRUNCHY PEANUT BUTTER BALLS

¼ cup chunky peanut butter
6 tblsp crushed No-sugar corn flakes
¼ cup scant 2% milk
2 tsp vanilla
¼ cup chopped raisins
Non-Saccharin sweetener to = 3 tsp sugar
1/3 cup moist coconut (see index)

COMBINE all ingredients except coconut . . .

FORM 12 balls and roll in coconut. CHILL.

APPROXIMATE EXCHANGE: 3 Balls = 1/2 Bread — 1/2 Meat — 1/2 Fruit — 1½ Fat

# CRUNCHY BANANA BALLS

1 small banana, beat to paste
1½ cup raisins, ground coarse
¼ cup nuts, chopped fine
6 tblsp moist coconut (see index)
Non-Saccharin sweetener to = ¼ cup sugar
1 tsp cinnamon
3 cups No-sugar corn flakes, Crushed to about ¾ cup crumbs

MIX TOGETHER banana, raisins, nuts, coconut, sweetener & cinnamon.

ROLL into 24 balls and roll in crumbs.

STORE in freezer.

APPROXIMATE EXCHANGE: 1 Ball = 1/4 Bread — 1/2 Fruit — 1/4 Fat

# CARROT CAROB CANDY

½ cup nuts, chop very fine
½ cup raw carrots, ground fine
¼ cup dry milk powder
2 tsp carob powder
¼ tsp cinnamon
Non-Saccharin sweetener to = 7 tsp sugar
¼ cup moist coconut (see index)

COMBINE nuts, carrots, milk powder, carob, cinnamon & sweetener until moist.

DROP by spoons full into coconut & form into 12 balls.

CHILL in freezer to hard . . . STORE in refrigerator.

APPROXIMATE EXCHANGE: 1 Ball = Trace of each — Bread, Milk & "B" or #2 Vegetable & 2/3 Fat

# APPLE BUTTER

8 small apples, peeled & sliced
¾ cup hot water
½ tblsp lemon juice
1 tsp cinnamon
¼ tsp cloves
$1/8$ tsp allspice
Non-Saccharin sweetener to = $2/3$ cup sugar or to taste

IN LARGE PAN combine apples and water. COOK about 20 minutes to tender.

REMOVE from heat and mash well.

ADD lemon juice, cinnamon, cloves and allspice. COOK slowly until thick; About 45 minutes stirring frequently.

COOL and add sweetener; STORE IN FREEZER.

APPROXIMATE EXCHANGE: 1 tsp trace Fruit

# APPLE JELLY

2 tsp unflavored gelatin
1 cup unsweetened apple juice
¾ tsp lemon juice
few drops yellow food coloring
Non-Saccharin sweetener to = $1/3$ cup sugar or to taste

SOFTEN gelatin in 1/4 cup cool juice.

BRING rest of juice to boil. REMOVE from burner and add gelatin stirring until dissolved.

ADD lemon juice, coloring & sweetener.

STORE in refrigerator and use within short time.

APPROXIMATE EXCHANGE: 4 tblsp = 3/4 Fruit

# CHERRY JAM

1½ cup canned unsweetened cherries, drained
¾ cup cherry juice
3 tsp gelatin
1½ tsp red food coloring
¾ tsp almond flavoring
1½ tsp cherry flavoring
Non-Saccharin sweetener to = ½ cup sugar


BLEND cherries to smooth and place in saucepan.

ADD juice, gelatin and simmer to dissolve gelatin.

SET OFF HEAT and add coloring and flavorings.

COOL 20 minutes and add sweetener.

STORE in refrigerator and use within short time.

APPROXIMATE EXCHANGE: 1 Tsp = Trace Fruit

# PINEAPPLE CHERRY JAM

1 cup canned unsweet cherries, drained
1 cup canned unsweet crushed pineapple, drained
½ cup pineapple juice
2 tsp unflavored gelatin
1 tsp red food coloring
Non-Saccharin sweetener to = $1/3$ to ½ cup sugar
    depending on sweetness desired

BLEND cherries & pineapple to smooth. POUR INTO saucepan &
add juice, gelatin and coloring.

COOK over low heat about 3 minutes to dissolve gelatin. SET off
heat 20 minutes. ADD sweetener.

STORE in refrigerator and use within short time.

APPROXIMATE EXCHANGE: 1 tsp = Trace Fruit

# DATE NUT SPREAD

1 cup pitted chopped dates
1 cup water
1 tsp lemon juice
1 tsp cinnamon
¼ cup nuts, chopped very fine

COOK dates, water and juice. MASH or blend until smooth. ADD cinnamon and nuts.

USE for rolls, cake fillings or spread on slices of warm tea bread.

APPROXIMATE EXCHANGE: 1/4 of Recipe = 4 Fruit — 3/4 Fat

# ORANGE SPREAD

$^2/_3$ cup dry milk powder
¼ cup orange juice
¼ tsp orange extract
Non-Saccharin sweetener to = 4 tsp sugar
$^1/_3$ cup soft butter

COMBINE milk powder, juice, extract and sweetener. STIR to dissolve milk powder.

PLACE in blender with butter and blend to smooth.

STORE in refrigerator.

USE as spread for tea breads, muffins, toast or cakes.

# STRAWBERRY BUTTER

2 tblsp butter, Very soft but not melted
¼ cup chopped fresh strawberries
Non-Saccharin sweetener to = 2 tsp sugar
½ tsp cinnamon
Red food coloring as desired

COMBINE all ingredients and beat on high until creamy.

# DRIED FRUIT JAM

4 whole dried apricots
10 medium prunes, pitted
8 whole dates, pitted
¼ cup raisins
Non-Saccharin sweetener to = 3 to 4 tblsp sugar
or to taste


GRIND fruit on coarse. SIMMER in small amount of water about 10 minutes to thick.

COOL and add sweetener.

STORE in freezer.

APPROXIMATE EXCHANGE: 1 tblsp = ¾ Fruit


# PRUNE BUTTER

20 medium prunes, chopped
½ cup undiluted frozen apple juice concentrate
½ tsp cinnamon
Non-Saccharin sweetener to = 2 tblsp sugar


SIMMER prunes in juice to tender, about 5 minutes; BLEND in blender to thick.

ADD cinnamon & sweetener.

STORE IN FREEZER.

APPROXIMATE EXCHANGE: 1 tblsp = ¾ Fruit

# PUMPKIN BUTTER

2½ cups cubed pared raw pumpkin
¾ cup apple juice
¼ cup orange juice
¾ tsp cinnamon
$1/8$ tsp cloves
$1/8$ tsp allspice
Non-Saccharin sweetener to = 3 tblsp sugar

HEAT pumpkin, apple juice & orange juice in non-stick saucepan & to boiling; Reduce heat and simmer, uncovered, until tender about 20 or 30 minutes.

REMOVE from heat and puree in blender until the consistency of applesauce.

HEAT mixture to boiling and reduce heat. Simmer, stirring occasionally until mixture will mound on spoon, about 2 hours.

STIR in cinnamon, cloves & allspice & simmer 15 minutes stirring frequently to avoid scorching. Cool slightly & add sweetener.

Store in freezer & take out only amount needed for a few days at a time.

APPROXIMATE EXCHANGE: Complete Recipe = $2^2/_3$ Bread — 3 Fruit

# RHUBARB SPREAD

COOK 2 cups rhubarb in 1/2 cup water to tender. ADD 2 tblsp pectin powder and cook 2 minutes.

COOL 20 minutes & add Non-Saccharin sweetener to taste.

STORE in freezer.

# STRAWBERRY JAM

1 cup strawberries, fresh or frozen unsweet
1 tsp unflavored gelatin
1 tblsp cold water
Non-Saccharin sweetener to = 4 tsp sugar

BLEND strawberries to smooth.

IN SAUCEPAN combine berries, gelatin & water.

HEAT and cook until gelatin is dissolved, about 1 minute.

Cool to lukewarm and add sweetener.

STORE in refrigerator & use in short time.

APPROXIMATE EXCHANGE: 1 tsp = Trace Fruit

# GRAPE JELLY

1½ cups unsweetened grape juice
1 envelope unflavored gelatin
½ cup water
1 cinnamon stick
2 whole cloves
Non-Saccharin sweetener to = $1/3$ cup sugar or to taste.

IN SAUCEPAN: Combine juice, gelatin, water & add cinnamon stick & cloves.

HEAT & cook at rolling boil about 1 minute.

REMOVE from heat and let cool 20 minutes.

REMOVE cinnamon stick & cloves and add sweetener.

STORE in refrigerator & use in short time.

APPROXIMATE EXCHANGE: 1 tblsp = 1/4 Fruit

# DESSERTS

Gelatins • Frozen Dessert
Ice Cream • Puddings • Toppings
Moist Coconut • Raisin Water

# FRESH FRUIT GELATIN

1 envelope unflavored gelatin
Dash Salt
1½ cups water
2 tblsp lemon juice
Non-Saccharin sweetener to
= ¼ cup sugar

1 small banana, peeled &
    chopped
1 small apple, peel, core and
    chop fine
½ cup white seedless grapes,
    cut up
¼ cup cantalope, chop fine

MIX gelatine, salt and ½ cup water in saucepan. On low heat stir until gelatine is dissolved.

REMOVE from heat and add 1 cup water, sweetener, and coloring. CHILL to slightly thickened.

ADD Fruits. Stir and chill. Serve with whipped topping.

APPROXIMATE EXCHANGE: 1/8 of recipe = 3/4 fruit exchange

# CRANBERRY PINEAPPLE GELATIN

1 envelope unflavored gelatin
¼ cup cold water
¾ cup crushed, water packed pineapple
    drain and save ½ cup of the juice
1 cup fresh frozen cranberries, coarse grind
½ cup orange juice
Non-Saccharin sweetener to = $1/3$ cup sugar

SOFTEN gelatin in water. COMBINE pineapple and cranberries in saucepan and heat to almost boiling.

STIR in gelatin; ADD pineapple juice and orange juice. Add sweetener.

POUR into a mold and chill to set.

APPROXIMATE EXCHANGE: 1/8 of recipe = 1/2 fruit exchange.

# ORANGE GELATIN

2½ tsp gelatin
1¼ cup orange juice
2 tsp lemon juice
Non-Saccharin sweetener to = ¼ cup sugar
1 small banana, chopped
1 small orange, cut up fine

SOFTEN gelatin in 1/4 cup orange juice.

HEAT 1 cup orange juice and add gelatin until dissolved completely. REMOVE from heat.

ADD lemon juice & cool . . . ADD sweetener and chill to slightly thickened . . .

ADD banana and orange and chill.

APPROXIMATE EXCHANGE: 1/4 of Recipe = $1\frac{1}{3}$ Fruit

# PINEAPPLE GELATIN

3¼ tsp gelatin
¾ cup water
3 tsp lemon juice
1 cup pineapple juice
¾ cup crushed pineapple, drained well
Few drops of yellow food coloring
Non-Saccharin sweetener to = ¼ cup sugar

SOFTEN gelatin in 1/4 cup water . . . MIX 1/2 cup water, lemon juice & pineapple juice and heat. ADD gelatin and cook until dissolved completely.

ADD pineapple and coloring and let cool.

ADD sweetener and chill. STIR before set completely to distribute fruit evenly.

APPROXIMATE EXCHANGE: 1/5 of Recipe = 1 Fruit

# VANILLA ICE CREAM

1 cup whole milk
2 medium eggs
Dash salt to taste
2 cups light cream
2 tsp vanilla
Non-Saccharin sweetener to = ¼ cup sugar or to taste

SCALD milk in double boiler.

BEAT eggs & salt and pour slowly into hot milk stirring constantly.

COOK until mixture coats spoon.

SET OFF heat and cool. ADD cream, vanilla, and sweetener.

POUR into freezing container and freeze.

BEAT with electric beater several times during freezing. SERVE at soft freeze.

APPROXIMATE EXCHANGE: 1/12 of Recipe = 1/5 Milk — 1½ Fat

# PEANUT BUTTER ICE CREAM

FOLLOW instructions for vanilla Ice cream.

COMBINE & beat to smooth 1/4 cup chunky peanut butter & 2 tblsp milk.

JUST before serving Ice cream fold peanut butter in until just blended.

NOTE: If ice cream becomes too hard in freezing: Let set out 15 minutes. Break up into chunks and beat with electric beater just before serving.

# BLUEBERRY ICE CREAM

PREPARE vanilla Ice cream recipe and add 1 cup fresh Blueberries after last beating.

# CHERRY ICE CREAM

BLEND 1 cup canned drained, unsweet cherries, 1/4 tsp almond flavoring, 1/4 tsp red food coloring and Non-Saccharin sweetener to = 2 tblsp sugar.

PREPARE vanilla Ice cream recipe and fold cherry mixture in after Ice cream has been frozen to mushy. Continue freezing.

# STRAWBERRY ICE CREAM

Thaw 1 cup frozen strawberries and whirl in blender until smooth. ADD sweetener to taste and fold into vanilla Ice cream just before freezing. Freeze as directed.

# BANANA NUT ICE CREAM

MASH 2 small bananas with a dash of lemon juice and a dash of nutmeg.

PREPARE vanilla Ice cream recipe and add banana mixture. Fold in 1/4 cup fine chopped peanuts. FREEZE as directed in recipe.

# PEACH ICE CREAM

MASH 1 or 2 fresh peaches and fold into vanilla Ice cream recipe. Freeze as directed.

# CHOCOLATE ICE CREAM

1 tblsp cornstarch
Dash of salt
½ cup water
Non-Saccharin sweetener to = ½ cup sugar
¾ cup Evaporated whole milk, Chilled
½ tsp vanilla
1 Square unsweetened chocolate, melted & cool
1 cup heavy cream, Whipped

DISSOLVE cornstarch & salt in water. COOK until boiling and thick stiring constantly.

COOL in refrigerator & add sweetener.

WHIP chilled evaporated milk to thick & add cornstarch mixture & vanilla.

FOLD IN chocolate & whipped cream together enough to blend.

POUR INTO freezing containers, cover & freeze.

APPROXIMATE EXCHANGE: 1/8 of Recipe = 1/5 Bread — 1/5 Milk — 2¾ Fat

# ORANGE SHERBET

1 small can (5½ oz) whole evaporated milk
5 tblsp unsweetened frozen orange juice concentrate, thawed
Non-Saccharin sweetener to = 5 tblsp sugar

CHILL milk and beat to stiff. GRADUALLY ADD orange juice and sweetener.

FREEZE in covered containers.

MAKES 3 cups.

APPROXIMATE EXCHANGE: 1/2 cup = 1/5 milk — 1/2 Fruit — 1/5 Fat

# STRAWBERRY MILKSHAKE

¼ cup plain yogurt
¼ cup 2% milk
½ tsp vanilla
Non-Saccharin sweetener to = 8 tsp sugar or to taste
²/₃ cup frozen strawberries, cut up
1 crushed ice cube
¼ cup vanilla ice cream (see index)

IN BLENDER place yogurt, milk, vanilla & sweetener and blend well.

ADD berries & ice and blend at high speed.

POUR into serving glass and add spoons of ice cream.

SERVE IMMEDIATELY.

APPROXIMATE EXCHANGE: 1/3 Bread — 3/4 Milk — 1 Fruit — 1¾ Fat

# ORANGE POPSICLE

MIX fresh or frozen orange juice with Non-Saccharin sweetener to desired taste.

POUR into popsicle molds and freeze solid.

VARIATION: USE apple or pineapple juice in place of orange juice.

# BANANA PINEAPPLE FROZEN DESSERT

1 cup whole evaporated milk
¾ cups crushed, unsweet Pineapple with juice
¼ cup orange juice
2 small bananas, Mashed
1½ tsp vanilla
¼ tsp Black walnut extract (optional)
Non-Saccharin sweetener to = 10 tsp sugar

PLACE milk in mixing bowl and place in freezer until crystals form around edges.

MEANWHILE:

IN BLENDER: Blend pineapple & juice to smooth.

COMBINE pineapple, bananas, vanilla, extract and sweetener and mix well.

BEAT evaporated milk until stiff peaks form.

STIR in pineapple mixture and place in freezer.

STIR often and serve when consistency of soft freeze.

APPROXIMATE EXCHANGE: 1/6 of Recipe = 1/3 Milk — 1 Fruit — 2/3 Fat


IF FROZEN too hard; Remove from freezer and let set about 20 minutes and beat to mushy before serving.

# PINEAPPLE FROZEN DESSERT

1 cup whole Evaporated milk
1 cup crushed unsweet pineapple with juice
¼ cup orange juice
1 tsp vanilla
Non-Saccharin sweetener to = ¼ cup sugar

POUR milk in mixing bowl and place in freezer until crystals form around edges.

MEANWHILE:
BLEND pineapple & juice to smooth.

ADD vanilla and sweetener, mixing well.

BEAT milk until stiff peaks form

MIX in pineapple mixture and place in freezer.

BEAT often until soft freeze consistency.

APPROXIMATE EXCHANGE: 1/4 of Recipe = 1/2 Fruit — 1/2 Milk — 1 Fat

NOTE: If frozen too hard; Remove from freezer and let set about 20 minutes.

BEAT until mushy and serve immediately.

# STRAWBERRY FROZEN DESSERT

¾ cup whole evaporated milk
1½ cups frozen unsweet strawberries, cut up
1 tsp vanilla
¼ cup 2% milk
Non-Saccharin sweetener to = 8 tsp sugar or taste

POUR milk in mixing bowl and place in freezer until crystals form around edges.

MEANWHILE:
COMBINE berries, vanilla, 2% milk and sweetener. BLEND to smooth.

BEAT Evaporated milk to stiff; FOLD in berries and place in freezer. Beat often until frozen to soft freeze.

APPROXIMATE EXCHANGE: 1/4 of Recipe = 1/2 Milk — 1/2 Fruit — 3/4 Fat

NOTE: If frozen too hard . . . Let set out for about 20 minutes and then beat to mushy. SERVE.

# CHERRY FROZEN DESSERT

DRAIN 1 (16 oz) can of unsweet red sour cherries and blend to smooth.

ADD ¼ tsp cherry flavoring, ¼ tsp red food coloring & Non-Saccharin sweetener to = 8 tsp sugar. FOLD into ¾ cup beaten evaporated milk.

FOLLOW instructions as for Strawberry dessert.

# APPLE PUDDING

1/3 cup raisins
2/3 cup water
2 small apples, Peeled and sliced thin
2 tsp cornstarch
3 tblsp water
1/2 tsp cinnamon
dash of salt
1/3 cup grapenuts
2 tblsp nuts, chop fine


IN SAUCEPAN: Simmer raisins in 2/3 cup water for about 5 minutes.

ADD apples and continue cooking until apples are tender.

MIX cornstarch in 3 tblsp water and add to apples and cook to thick.

ADD cinnamon, salt and one half of grapenuts.

POUR into casserole dish. SPRINKLE top with rest of grapenuts and the nuts.

BAKE 325 degrees 15 minutes.

WHILE still warm divide into dessert dishes.

Top with Whip topping.

MAKES 8 servings.

APPROXIMATE EXCHANGE: 1 Serving = 2/3 Fruit — 1/5 Fat

# PINEAPPLE TAPIOCA PUDDING

2 tblsp tapioca
dash salt
½ cup water
½ cup pinapple juice, unsweet
½ cup crushed
unsweet pineapple

1 tblsp orange juice concentrate
¼ tsp vanilla
½ tsp pineapple extract
Non-Saccharin sweetener to
= 3 tblsp sugar

IN SAUCEPAN mix tapioca, salt, water & pineapple juice. COOK slowly until clear stirring frequently. REMOVE from heat.

ADD pineapple, orange concentrate, vanilla & pineapple extract. Stir well & add sweetener.

CHILL & serve with whip topping (see index).

APPROXIMATE EXCHANGE: 1/3 of Recipe = 1 Fruit plus topping used.

# ORANGE TAPIOCA PUDDING

1¼ cup Orange juice
2 tblsp quick tapioca
dash salt
1 small peeled sweet orange, Cut up
Non-Saccharin sweetener to = 12 tsp sugar or to taste

IN SAUCEPAN: Mix orange juice & tapioca & let set 5 minutes. BRING to boil & cook until tapioca is clear.

LET set off heat 20 minutes. ADD orange pieces and sweetener. CHILL before serving.

APPROXIMATE EXCHANGE: 1/2 Recipe = 1/4 Bread — 1¾ Fruit

# CHOCOLATE PUDDING

3 tblsp cornstarch
$1/_8$ tsp salt
2½ cup 2% milk
1 Sq. unsweetened chocolate, melted
3 tsp butter
½ tsp Chocolate flavoring
1 tsp vanilla
Non-Saccharin sweetener to = 6½ tblsp sugar

MIX cornstarch, salt & 1/2 cup cold milk

SCALD 2 cups milk in double boiler and add cornstarch mixture.

COOK until slightly thickened.

ADD chocolate and butter. REMOVE from heat.

ADD chocolate and vanilla flavorings.

COOL 10 minutes and then add sweetener.

CHILL and serve within 2 days with whip topping.

APPROXIMATE EXCHANGE: 1/5 of Recipe = 1/2 Bread — 1/2 Milk — 1⅓ Fat PLUS topping

# CHERRY TOPPING

2 tsp cornstarch
½ cup cherry juice, unsweet from cherries
1 cup canned unsweet red sour cherries, drained
¼ tsp almond extract
$1/8$ tsp red food coloring
Non-Saccharin sweetener to = 2 tblsp sugar

IN SAUCEPAN: Dissolve cornstarch in juice. HEAT and add cherries; Cook to clear.

REMOVE from heat & let set 20 minutes. ADD rest of ingredients and cool.

USE as topping for cakes, Ice cream or puddings.

FOR USE WITH cream pie filling; Layer in crumb crust with filling; sprinkle top with crumbs and chill. Serve within 2 days.

APPROXIMATE EXCHANGE: 1/4 of Recipe = 3/4 Fruit

# PINEAPPLE TOPPING OR FILLING

3 tblsp cornstarch
2 cups crushed unsweetened pineapple with juice
Non-Saccharin sweetener to = ¼ cup sugar

COMBINE in saucepan the cornstarch and pineapple with juice. HEAT and cook over low heat to thick stirring constantly.

REMOVE from heat and cool to lukewarm. ADD sweetener.

SPREAD over cream pie filling or use as filling for cakes.

APPROXIMATE EXCHANGE: 1/8 of this Recipe = 1/4 Bread — 1/2 Fruit

# BLUEBERRY TOPPING

1 cup blueberries, fresh or frozen unsweet
3 tblsp water
½ tblsp lemon juice
2 tsp cornstarch
¼ tsp vannila
Non-sweetener to = 8 tsp sugar

COMBINE 1/2 cup blueberries, 2 tblsp water & lemon juice and bring to boiling.

MIX cornstarch & 1 tblsp water and add to hot berries. Cook to thick. Add vanilla & cook few minutes. SET off heat and add rest of berries. STIR well and add sweetener.

COOL and spread over top of cream filling (see index)

CHILL and serve within 2 days.

APPROXIMATE EXCHANGE: 1/8 of Recipe = 1/3 Fruit

# STRAWBERRY TOPPING

1¼ cup strawberries, frozen & unsweetened
3 tblsp water
2 tsp cornstarch
½ tsp vanilla
Non-Saccharin sweetener to = ¼ cup sugar

Heat 2 tblsp water. Mix 1 tblsp water & cornstarch and add to hot water. Stir to thicken. Add vanilla and cook to thick.

ADD 1/2 cup small or sliced thick berries. Cook just to heat through stirring carefully.

REMOVE from heat & fold in 1/2 cup berries. Cool to room temperature & add sweetener.

IN prepared crumb crust slice 1/4 cup berries then spread in cream filling. Top with cooked berry mixture. CHILL.

APPROXIMATE EXCHANGE: 1/8 of Recipe = 1/3 Fruit

# MOIST COCONUT

1 tsp butter, melted
1 tsp water
Non-Saccharin sweetener to = 3 tsp sugar
¾ cup unsweetened coconut

ADD butter to water & then add sweetener & stir until dissolved.

POUR over coconut . . . STIR well . . . STORE in closed jar in refrigerator and use where recipe requests MOIST COCONUT.

APPROXIMATE EXCHANGE: 1/4 Cup = 3/4 Bread — 1¾ Fat :

NOTE: IF recipe requests MOIST COCONUT #2 . . . PREPARE above recipe eliminating the sweetener.

# RAISIN WATER

1 cup water
$1/3$ cup raisins

HEAT water and add raisins. SIMMER 5 minutes.

DRAIN & use water in recipes as needed. . . . USE raisins in cakes and cookies.

# PIES

# BANANA CREAM PIE

2 cups skim milk
6 tblsp conrstarch
¼ tsp salt
3 egg yolks, slightly beaten
¾ tsp vanilla
Non-Saccharin sweetener to = 3 tblsp sugar
2 small bananas, sliced

1 - 9" prepared Crumb or Corn flake crust (see index)


IN NON-STICK SAUCEPAN or Double boiler, Scald 1½ cup milk.

MIX TOGETHER 1/2 cup cold milk, cornstarch & salt . . . ADD slowly to hot milk stirring constantly with whisk to slightly thickened.

ADD little of hot mixture to yolks and then stir into hot mixture. Continue cooking & stirring with whip until mixture is thick.

REMOVE from heat & add vanilla . . . Cool slightly and add sweetener.

In shell, layer pudding & bananas, starting & ending with pudding.

TOP with crumbs & sprinkle lightly with cinnamon . . . CHILL. Serve within 2 or 3 days.

APPROXIMATE EXCHANGE: 1/8 Pie = 1/2 Bread — 1/4 Milk — 1/2 Fruit — 1/5 Meat — 1/5 Fat Plus Crust exchange

# BANANA CUSTARD PIE

1 envelope plain gelatin
1¾ cups skim milk
1 egg, slightly beaten
3 small ripe bananas
1½ tsp vanilla
1 tblsp orange juice
½ tsp orange extract
½ tsp salt
Non-Saccharin sweetener to = 4 tsp sugar


Heat 1 cup milk over hot water. Soften gelatin in 3/4 cup milk and add to hot milk until dissolved. ADD egg and mix thoroughly.

COOK over hot water until mixture begins to thicken, stirring constantly.

REMOVE from heat and add 2 mashed bananas, vanilla, orange juice and orange extract & salt.

COOL slightly and add sweetener. Let cool to slightly thickened.

SLICE 1 banana in bottom of prepared Corn flake crust (see index). Sprinkle top with crumbs and cinnamon. CHILL before serving.

APPROXIMATE EXCHANGE: 1/8 Pie = 1/3 Bread — 1/5 Milk — 3/4 Fruit — 1⅔ Fat

# COCONUT CREAM PIE

2 tsp butter, melted
1 cup unsweetened coconut
Non-Saccharin sweetener to = 3 tblsp sugar
2 cups skim milk
4½ tblsp cornstarch
¼ tsp salt
3 egg yolks, slightly beaten
½ tsp vanilla

1 - 9" prepared pastry of your choice (see index)


POUR melted butter over coconut & add sweetener to = 1 tblsp sugar. SET ASIDE.

IN NON-STICK SAUCEPAN or Double boiler, Scald 1½ cup milk.

MIX TOGETHER 1/2 cup cold milk, cornstarch and salt . . . ADD slowly to hot milk stirring constantly with whisk & cook to thickened.

ADD little of hot mixture to yolks & then stir into hot mixture . . Continue cooking & stirring with whip until mixture is thick.

REMOVE from heat & add vanilla . . . Cool slightly and add rest of sweetener . . . ADD coconut.

POUR into prepared pastry shell & sprinkle top with cinnamon as desired . . . CHILL. Serve within 2 or 3 days.

APPROXIMATE EXCHANGE: 1/8 Pie = 2/3 Bread — 1/4 Milk — 1/5 Meat — 1¹/₅ Fat Plus Pastry

# CREAM CHEESE LEMON PIE

¼ cup cornstarch
1 cup water
2 egg yolks, slightly beaten
3 oz (6 tblsp) cream cheese
$1/3$ cup lemon juice
Non-Saccharin sweetener to = 9 tblsp sugar
3 egg whites stiffly beaten

IN SAUCEPAN mix water and cornstarch.

WHISK in yolks and cook over low heat to thick, stirring with whisk constantly.

STIR in cream cheese until melted.

REMOVE from heat and add lemon.

COOL 10 minutes and then add sweetener.

FOLD in beaten egg whites gently.

POUR into baked 9" pastry or crumb crust of your choice and chill.

SERVE within 2 days.

MAKES 8 servings.

APPROXIMATE EXCHANGE: 1 Serving = 1/3 Bread — 1/10 Fruit — 1/3 Meat — 1 Fat PLUS pastry or crumb crust

# CREAM PIE FILLING

2 cups 2% milk
5 tblsp cornstarch
¼ tsp salt
3 egg yolks, slightly beaten
¾ tsp vanilla
Non-Saccharin sweetener to = 3 tbslp sugar

1 - 9" prepared crumb or corn flake crust


IN NON-STICK SAUCEPAN or Double boiler, Scald 1½ cup milk.

MIX TOGETHER 1/2 cup cold milk, cornstarch and salt . . . ADD slowly to hot milk stirring constantly with whisk to slightly thick.

ADD little hot mixture to yolks and then stir into hot mixture and continue cooking and stirring until mixture is thick.

REMOVE from heat and add vanilla . . . cool to lukewarm and add sweetener.

POUR into prepared crust and top with either Blueberry, strawberry, pineapple or cherry topping (see Index).

APPROXIMATE EXCHANGE: 1/8 Pie = 1/2 Bread — 1/4 Milk — 1/5 Meat — 1/2 Fat Plus Crust and any topping

# FROZEN CHOCOLATE COCONUT PIE

½ cup 2% milk
½ cup dates, chopped fine (about 16 dates)
1½ tsp cornstarch
2 tblsp cocoa
$1/_8$ tsp salt
1 medium egg yolk
½ cup moist coconut (see Index)
1 tsp vanilla
Non-Saccharin sweetener to = ¼ cup sugar
½ cup low fat evaporated milk, chilled
1 corn flake crust (see Index)

IN SAUCEPAN: MIX milk and dates & cook until dates are soft. Mash up the dates with the milk and set aside.

MIX cornstarch, cocoa and salt. Set date mixture back on stove and slowly add cornstarch mixture using a whip.

BEAT egg yolk and add to hot mixture mixing quickly. COOK to thick stirring constantly.

SET off heat and add coconut and vanilla.

COOL slightly and add sweetener.

LET COOL TO ROOM TEMPERATURE.

BEAT well chilled evaporated milk until stiff and fold into chocolate mixture.

POUR into flake crust and top with rest of the crumbs. FREEZE to solid before serving.

APPROXIMATE EXCHANGE: 1/8 Pie = 1/3 Bread — 1 Fruit — Trace Milk — 1/2 Fat — PLUS CRUST

# FUDGY
# COCONUT CREAM PIE

2 cups skim milk
5 tblsp cornstarch
¼ tsp salt
3 egg yolks, slightly beaten
½ tsp vanilla
2 Sq. unsweet chocolate, Melted
Non-Saccharin sweetener to = 6 tblsp sugar
½ cup moist coconut (see index)

1 - 9″ prepared Corn flake crumb crust (see index)

IN NON-STICK SAUCEPAN or Double boiler, scald 1½ cup milk.

MIX TOGETHER 1/2 cup cold milk, cornstarch & salt . . . ADD slowly to hot milk stirring constantly with whisk to slightly thickened.

ADD little of hot mixture to yolks and then stir into hot mixture. Continue cooking and stirring with whip until mixture is thick.

REMOVE from heat & add vanilla & chocolate.

COOL slightly and add sweetener & coconut.

POUR into crust & top with crumbs from crust recipe . . . CHILL. Serve within 2 or 3 days.

APPROXIMATE EXCHANGE: 1/8 Pie = 1/2 Bread — 1/4 Milk — 1/4 Fruit — 1/5 Meat — 1⅓ Fat Plus Crust exchange

# MAPLE COCONUT CREAM PIE

2 cups skim milk
5 tblsp cornstarch
¼ tsp salt
3 egg yolks, slightly beaten
½ tsp vanilla
3 tsp maple flavoring
Non-saccharin sweetener to = 8 tsp sugar
½ cup moist coconut (see index)
¼ cup nuts, chopped
1 - 9" prepared Corn flake crumb crust (see index)


IN NON-STICK SAUCEPAN or Double boiler, Scald 1½ cup milk.

MIX TOGETHER 1/2 cup cold milk, cornstarch & salt . . . ADD slowly to hot milk stirring constantly with whisk to slightly thickened.

ADD little of hot mixture to yolks and then stir into hot mixture. Continue cooking & stirring with whip until mixture is thick.

REMOVE from heat & add vanilla & Maple flavoring . . . Cool slightly and add sweetener, coconut & nuts.

POUR into crust & top with crumbs. CHILL.

Serve within 2 or 3 days.

APPROXIMATE EXCHANGE: 1/8 Pie = 1/2 Bread — 1/4 Milk — 1/5 Meat — 1 Fat Plus Crust exchange

# PEACH CREAM PIE

2 cups skim milk
6 tblsp cornstarch
¼ tsp salt
3 egg yolks, slightly beaten
½ tsp vanilla
1 tsp almond flavoring
Non-Saccharin sweetener to = ¼ cup sugar
2 cups cups canned, water packed peaches

SEVERAL HOURS IN ADVANCE: Cut up peaches & warm in juice just to cover . . . Set off heat & add 1/2 tsp almond flavor & sweetener to = 4 tsp sugar. Let set room temperature. Can be refrigerated overnight if desired.


IN NON-STICK SAUCEPAN or Double boiler; Scald 1½ cup milk.

MIX TOGETHER 1/2 cup cold milk, cornstarch & salt . . . ADD slowly to hot milk stirring constantly with whisk to slightly thickened.

ADD little hot mixture to yolks and then stir into hot mixture. Continue cooking & stirring with whip until mixture is thick.

REMOVE from heat & add vanilla, 1/2 tsp almond flavor. Cool slightly then add rest of sweetener.

DRAIN peaches very well and add to creamed mixture. Pour into prepared 9" crumb or flake crust (see index). Sprinkle crumbs on top.

CHILL . . . Serve within 2 or 3 days.

APPROXIMATE EXCHANGE: 1/8 Pie = 1/2 Bread — 1/4 Milk — 1/2 Fruit — 1/5 Meat — 1/5 Fat Plus Crust exchange

# PEANUT BUTTER CREAM PIE

2½ cup skim milk
½ cup flour
¼ tsp salt
2 egg yolks, slightly beaten
½ tsp vanilla
½ cup crunchy peanut butter
Non-Saccharin sweetener to = ½ cup sugar


SCALD 1¾ cup milk in top of double boiler.

MIX flour & salt and stir into 1/2 cup cold milk, then add to hot milk & continue cooking 15 minutes, stirring often.

POUR some hot mixture over yolks, mix well then add to rest of hot mixture. COOK 3 minutes. COOL.

MIX rest of cold milk, vanilla, peanut butter & sweetener & beat to smooth. ADD cooked mixture and beat well. POUR into 9'' crumb or flake crust.

CHILL and serve with whipped topping.

SERVE within 3 days.

APPROXIMATE EXCHANGE: 1/8 Pie = 1/2 Bread — 1/4 Milk — 1/2 Meat — 1 Fat Plus Crust exchange.

# PINEAPPLE CREAM PIE

2 cups skim milk
5 tblsp cornstarch
¼ tsp salt
3 egg yolks, slightly beaten
½ tsp vanilla
1½ tsp Pineapple flavoring
Non-Saccharin sweetener to = ¼ cup sugar
2 cups water pack, crushed Pineapple (very well drained)

1 - 9" Crumb or Corn flake crust (see index)


PLACE drained pineapple in bowl & add sweetener to = 1 tblsp sugar and pineapple flavoring.
SET ASIDE.

IN NON-STICK SAUCEPAN or Double boiler: Scald 1½ cup milk.

MIX TOGETHER 1/2 cup cold milk, cornstarch & salt . . . ADD slowly to hot milk stirring constantly with a whip to slightly thickened.

ADD little of hot mixture to yolks and then stir into hot mixture. Continue cooking & stirring with whisk until mixture is thick.

REMOVE from heat & add vanilla . . . Cool slightly and add rest of sweetener. ADD pineapple.

POUR into shell & sprinkle crumbs on top . . . Sprinkle lightly with cinnamon . . . CHILL. Serve within 2 or 3 days.

APPROXIMATE EXCHANGE: 1/8 of Pie = 1/3 Bread — 1/4 milk — 1/2 Fruit — 1/5 Meat — 1/5 Fat Plus Pastry exchange.

# NO-BAKE PUMPKIN PIE

1½ tblsp unflavored gelatin
1½ cups whole milk
2 tblsp margarine
1¼ cup canned OR cooked & mashed pumpkin
½ tsp ginger
1 tsp cinnamon
½ tsp salt
Non-Saccharin sweetener to = $1/3$ cup sugar

DISSOLVE gelatin in 1/4 cup cold milk. HEAT 1¼ cup milk and add cold milk mixture, Cook to dissolved.

MIX pumpkin, spices and salt and add to hot mixture. ADD margarine and heat to melted.

REMOVE from heat and cool and add sweetener.

POUR into 9″ baked pastry shell and chill. Serve with whipped topping within 2 days.

APPROXIMATE EXCHANGE: 1/8 Recipe = 1/5 Milk — 1/5 "B" Vegetable #2 list — 1$1/10$ fat PLUS PASTRY EXCHANGE.

# WHIPPED TOPPING

½ cup skim instant dry milk powder
½ cup ice water
½ tsp lemon extract
½ tsp vanilla
Non-Saccharin sweetener to = 3 tblsp sugar

IN CHILLED BOWL blend all ingredients & then beat high speed to peaks.

APPROXIMATE EXCHANGE: 1/3 of Recipe = 1/2 milk exchange

# BREAD CRUMB CRUST

Wholewheat bread (No-sugar — commercially packed. Similar to
  Rusks or Zweiback)
  Crush to = 1 cup crumbs (about 4 slices)
3 tblsp melted butter
¼ cup chopped nuts
½ tsp cinnamon
Non-Saccharin sweetener to = 4 tsp sugar

MIX butter & sweetener and add to crumbs.

ADD rest of ingredients stiring in well . . .

IN 9" pie pan press about 2/3 of the mixture into bottom & sides.
Use pyrex pie pan to press in real well . . CHILL well before filling.

RESERVE rest of crumbs for top of pie.

APPROXIMATE EXCHANGE: 1/8 Crust = 1/2 Bread — 1½ Fat

# CORN FLAKE CRUST

2¼ cup No-sugar Corn flakes, Crushed to = 1 cup
3 tblsp butter, melted
Non-Saccharin sweetener to = 2 tsp sugar
½ tsp cinnamon
¼ cup nuts, chopped fine

MIX butter & sweetener — ADD to crumbs . . . ADD rest of ingredients and stir well.

PRESS about 2/3 of crumbs in bottom & sides of 9" pie shell using
another pie pan to press in real well . . . CHILL well before filling.

RESERVE rest of crumbs to sprinkle on top of pie.

APPROXIMATE EXCHANGE: 1/8 Crust = 1/3 Bread — 1½ Fat

# SALADS•SYRUPS

# SAUCES

# APPLESAUCE

8 small apples, cored & peeled & cut up
$1/3$ cup water
½ cup raisins, soaked in hot water & drained
1 tsp cinnamon, if desired
Non-Saccharin sweetener to = ¼ cup sugar

COOK apples in water to tender; Cool slightly and mash or force through food mill.

ADD raisins, cinnamon and sweetener.

MAKES about 4 cups applesauce. STORE IN FREEZER.

APPROXIMATE EXCHANGE: 1/2 cup = 1½ Fruit

NOTE: More raisins and sweetener may be added.

# CRANBERRY SAUCE

½ cup water
1½ cup fresh Cranberries
Non-Saccharin sweetener to = 5 tblsp sugar or to individual taste

Bring water to boiling . . . ADD berries & simmer until berries are soft . . . SET off heat to cool slightly . . . ADD sweetener.

STORE in refrigerator or freezer.

APPROXIMATE EXCHANGE: Small amounts free

# CRANBERRY APPLESAUCE

1 cup cooked strained cranberries, unsweetened
1 cup unsweet applesauce
Non-Saccharin sweetener to = ½ cup sugar
½ tsp cinnamon

COMBINE all ingredients. STORE in freezer. Thaw as used.

APPROXIMATE EXCHANGE: 1/2 cup = 1/4 Bread − 1/2 Fruit

# RHUBARB SAUCE

2 cups rhubarb, Cut up
¼ cup water
Non-Saccharin sweetener to taste

COOK rhubarb in water to tender. REMOVE from heat and cool.
ADD sweetener.

STORE in freezer or use within 2 days.

APPROXIMATE EXCHANGE: 1/2 cup = 1 "B" Vegetable

# STRAWBERRY SAUCE

1 tblsp water
1 cup strawberries, Frozen & thawed
½ tsp grated orange rind
1 tsp cornstarch
Non-Saccharin sweetener to = 1 tblsp sugar

IN SAUCEPAN: Combine water, berries, rind and cornstarch.
COOK over low heat to thick.

COOL and add sweetener.

STORE in refrigerator and use as topping on Ice cream, Puddings, etc.

APPROXIMATE EXCHANGE: 1/4 cup = 1/3 Fruit

# MAPLE SYRUP

1½ cups cold water
1 tblsp cornstarch
$^1/_8$ tsp salt
1 tsp maple flavoring
Non-Saccharin sweetener to = $^2/_3$ cup sugar

HEAT 1 cup water; Mix cornstarch in 1/2 cup cold water and add to hot water, stir well.

ADD salt & flavoring and bring to boil.

REMOVE from heat and cool. ADD sweetener.

CHILL & use in few days.

APPROXIMATE EXCHANGE: Complete recipe = 1/2 Bread

# BLUEBERRY SYRUP

½ cup cold water
2 tsp cornstarch
1 cup frozen unsweetened Blueberries
1 tsp lemon juice
Non-Saccharin sweetener to = ¼ cup sugar

IN SAUCEPAN: Combine water and cornstarch.

HEAT and add blueberries; Cook slow to thickened.

SET off heat and add lemon juice. COOL and add sweetener.

USE on waffles or pancakes.

APPROXIMATE EXCHANGE: 1/4 of recipe = 1/2 Fruit

# APPLE COCONUT SALAD

2 small apples
2 tblsp raisins, chopped
2 tblsp Moist coconut (see index)
1 tblsp Peanuts, chopped

Peel, core and chop the apples.

IN BOWL combine all ingredients.


# PEANUT BUTTER DRESSING

2 tblsp creamy peanut butter
2 to 3 tblsp milk
Non-Saccharin sweetener to = 1 tsp sugar or to taste
Dash of cinnamon to taste

BEAT peanut butter and milk to creamy.

ADD sweetener, and cinnamon. MIX well.

TOSS with fruit. SERVE chilled.

APPROXIMATE EXCHANGE: 1/3 of Recipe with dressing = 1 Fruit — 1/3 Meat — 1 Fat

*** If thicker dressing desired, add a little Yogurt and cream with peanut butter . . You may wish to cut down on amount of milk and add little more sweetener.

# CARROT APPLE SALAD

½ cup ground raw carrots
1 small apple, shredded
½ tsp cinnamon
1 tsp mayonnaise
Non-Saccharin sweetener to = 1 tsp sugar

TOSS TOGETHER carrots and apple . . MIX sweetener, cinnamon & mayonnaise and mix into salad. SERVE on lettuce leaf.

APPROXIMATE EXCHANGE: Complete recipe = 1 fruit — 1 "B" vegetable — 1 fat

# FRUIT & CABBAGE COLESLAW

1 cup cabbage, shredded
½ cup canned unsweetened pears, Drain & chop,
½ cup canned unsweetened peaches, Drain & chop,
¼ cup canned unsweetened pineapple, crushed
½ tsp salt
½ cup creamed cottage cheese

MIX all ingredients together. SERVE on bed of lettuce.

APPROXIMATE EXCHANGE: 1/5 of recipe = 1/2 Fruit — 1/2 Vegetable — 1/2 Meat — 1/5 Fat

NOTE: If preferred, 1 cup unsweetened fruit cocktail may be substituted for pears & peaches.

# CHICKEN & FRUIT SALAD

2 cups white chicken meat, Cooked & chopped
½ cup pineapple tidbits, drained
1 small apple, chopped fine
½ cup seedless grapes, cut up
¼ cup walnuts, chopped fine
Small amount of pineapple juice to moisten

COMBINE all ingredients. CHILL & serve on bed of lettuce.

APPROXIMATE EXCHANGE: 1/2 Cup = 1 Fruit — 3 Meat — 3/4 Fat Plus Mayonnaise if used.

* * * Small amount of mayonnaise may be added.

# FRUIT SALAD

½ small orange, chopped fine
2 small apples, finely chopped
2 small bananas, chopped
1 tblsp moist coconut (see index)
1 tblsp raisins, chopped
2 tblsp nuts, chopped
½ tsp cinnamon
2 tblsp whipping cream
Non-Saccharin sweetener to = 2 tsp sugar or to taste

COMBINE fruit, coconut, raisins, & nuts.

WHIP cream & add cinnamon & sweetener. FOLD into fruit.

SERVE immediately on lettuce leaves.

APPROXIMATE EXCHANGE: 1/2 Recipe = 3 Fruit — 2 Fat

# PINEAPPLE FRUIT SALAD

3 cups crushed, unsweet pineapple
12 dates
2 small bananas, chopped
2 cups small green grapes, chopped

DRAIN pineapple very well.

IN HOT WATER soak dates 5 minutes. DRAIN well and chop fine.

COMBINE all above ingredients and chill.

SERVE on bed of lettuce with Coconut dressing.


# COCONUT DRESSING

¼ cup orange juice
¼ cup pineapple juice (from crushed above)
¼ cup moist coconut (See index)
Non-Saccharin sweetener to = 2 tsp sugar

MIX all together and toss with fruit.

APPROXIMATE EXCHANGE: 1/12 of Recipe = $2^1/_5$ Fruit — 1/6 Fat

# PINEAPPLE DRESSING

¼ cup mayonnaise
6 tblsp pineapple juice
Non-Saccharin sweetener to = 3 tsp sugar or to taste
BLEND together and pour over coleslaw or fruit salad.

# BANANA DRESSING

1 small banana, chopped
¼ cup plain skim yogurt
1 tblsp lemon juice
Non-Saccharin sweetener to = 4 tsp sugar
BLAND together. POUR over fruit salad.
SPRINKLE with cinnamon if desired.

# ORANGE DRESSING

¼ cup orange juice
1 small banana, chopped
$^1/_3$ cup dates, chopped fine
Non-Saccharin sweetener to taste if desired
BLEND juice and banana to smooth. ADD dates and sweetener.
POUR OVER fruit salad . . . Sprinkle with cinnamon if desired.

# BANANA RAISIN DRESSING

1 small banana, chopped
¼ cup milk
½ cup raisins, chopped
Non-Saccharin sweetener to taste if desired
BLEND banana and milk. ADD raisins & sweetener. POUR over fruit salad.

# INDEX

BREADS . . . . . . . 7

    Apple filled yeast rolls . . 19
    Apple spice tea bread . . 9
    Blueberry tea bread . . . 10
    Blueberry orange bread . 16
    Cinnamon yeast rolls . . 18
    Date nut yeast rolls . . . 18
    Orange date tea bread . . 11
    Pineapple date tea bread . 12
    Prune tea bread . . . . 13
    Prune filled yeast rolls . . 19
    Raisin tea bread . . . . 14
    Whole wheat yeast rolls . 20
    Yeast rolls, basic recipe . 17

CAKES . . . . . . 21 - 32

    Applesauce . . . . 23
    Banana . . . . . . 24
    Cherry . . . . . . 25
    Chocolate coconut . . . 26
    Maple . . . . . . 27
    Orange raisin . . . . 28
    Orange gelatin . . . 29
    Pineapple juice . . . 30
    Pineapple . . . . . 31
    Prune . . . . . . 32

COCONUT (Moist) . . . . 72

COOKIES & BARS . . 34 - 44

    Almond cookies . . . . 38
    Apple date drops . . . . 36
    Apple bars . . . . . 43
    Applesauce cookies . . . 37
    Banana cookies . . . . 42
    Coconut macaroons . . . 37
    Fruit drops . . . . . 39
    Oatmeal bars . . . . . 44
    Orange cookies . . . . 40
    Maple date bars . . . . 44
    Pineapple cookies . . . 41
    Tomato cookies . . . . 42

CONFECTIONS . . . 47 - 49

    Apricot date balls . . . 47

CONFECTIONS (cont.)

    Banana balls . . . . . 49
    Coconut fruit balls . . . 47
    Cocoa fruit balls . . . . 48
    Carrot carob balls . . . 49
    Peanut butter balls . . . 48

DESSERTS, FROZEN . . . 64

    Banana Pineapple . . . 64
    Cherry . . . . . . 66
    Pineapple . . . . . . 65
    Strawberry . . . . . 66

FILLINGS . . . . . . 19

    Apple . . . . . . 19
    Prune . . . . . . 19

FROSTING . . . . 32 - 33

    Chocolate . . . . . 33
    Jelly . . . . . . . 33
    Prune . . . . . . 32

GELATINS. . . . 58 - 59

    Cranberry pineapple . . 58
    Fruit . . . . . . . 58
    Orange . . . . . . 59
    Pineapple . . . . . 59

ICE CREAM . . . 60 - 63

    Banana . . . . . . 61
    Blueberry . . . . . 61
    Cherry . . . . . . 61
    Chocolate . . . . . 62
    Orange sherbet . . . 62
    Peach . . . . . . 61
    Peanut Butter . . . . 61
    Strawberry . . . . . 61
    Vanilla . . . . . . 60

JAMS — JELLY — SPREADS 50

    Applebutter . . . . 50
    Apple jelly . . . . . 50
    Cherry jam . . . . . 51
    Date nut spread . . . . 52
    Dried fruit jam . . . . 53

# INDEX

JAMS - JELLY - SPREADS (cont.)

Grape jelly . . . . . 55
Orange spread . . . . . 52
Pineapple cherry jam . . 51
Prune butter . . . . . 53
Pumpkin butter . . . . 54
Rhubarb spread . . . 54
Strawberry butter . . . 52
Strawberry jam . . . . 55

MILKSHAKE
Strawberry . . . . . . 63

MUFFINS . . . . . . . 15
Apple . . . . . . . 15
Blueberry Orange . . . 16
Corn flake spice . . . . 16

PIES . . . . . . . . 73
Banana cream . . . . . 75
Banana custard . . . . 76
Chocolate, frozen . . . 80
Coconut cream . . . . 77
Coconut, fudgy . . . . 81
Coconut cream, maple . . 82
Cream pie, filling . . . . 79
Lemon, cream cheese . . 78
Peach cream . . . . . 83
Peanut butter cream . . 84
Pineapple cream . . . . 85
Pumpkin, no-bake . . . 86

PIE CRUST . . . . . . 87
Bread crumb . . . . . 87
Corn flake . . . . . . 87

POPSICLE . . . . . . . 63

PUDDINGS . . . . . . 67
Apple . . . . . . . 67
Chocolate . . . . . . 69

PUDDINGS (cont.)
Orange tapioca . . . . 68
Pineapple tapioca . . . 68

RAISIN WATER . . . . . 72

SALADS . . . . . . . 93
Apple coconut . . . 93
Carrot apple . . . . . 94
Chicken & fruit . . . . 95
Fruit . . . . . . . . 95
Fruit & cabbage . . . . 94
Pineapple fruit . . . . 96

SALAD DRESSINGS 93 - 96 - 97
Banana . . . . . . . 97
Banana raisin . . . . . 97
Coconut . . . . . . 96
Orange . . . . . . . 97
Pineapple . . . . . . 97
Peanut butter . . . . . 93

SAUCES . . . . . . . 90
Applesauce . . . . . 90
Cranberry . . . . . . 90
Cranberry applesauce . . 91
Strawberry . . . . . . 91
Rhubarb . . . . . . 91

SYRUPS . . . . . . . 92
Blueberry . . . . . . 92
Maple . . . . . . . 92

TOPPINGS . . . . . . 70
Blueberry . . . . . . 71
Cherry . . . . . . . 70
Pineapple . . . . . . 70
Strawberry . . . . . . 71
Whipped . . . . . . . 86

How to order additional copies of the

# NO-SUGAR
# COOKBOOK

Follow prices below for
amount of books wanted

Send Check or Money Order along with
Your Mailing Address to:

## AD-DEE PUBLISHERS, INC.

Drawer 5426 — SL83
Eugene, Oregon 97405

1 BOOK      $ 5.99
2 BOOKS     10.99
3 BOOKS     14.99
6 BOOKS     28.99

Postage paid direct to you.

Volume prices available to bookstores, fundraisers and dealers up-
on request.